JN440348

Suicide Parasite

Suicide Parasite

A collection of new poems by Kim Seong-gyu
Translated by YoungShil Ji, Daniel T. Parker

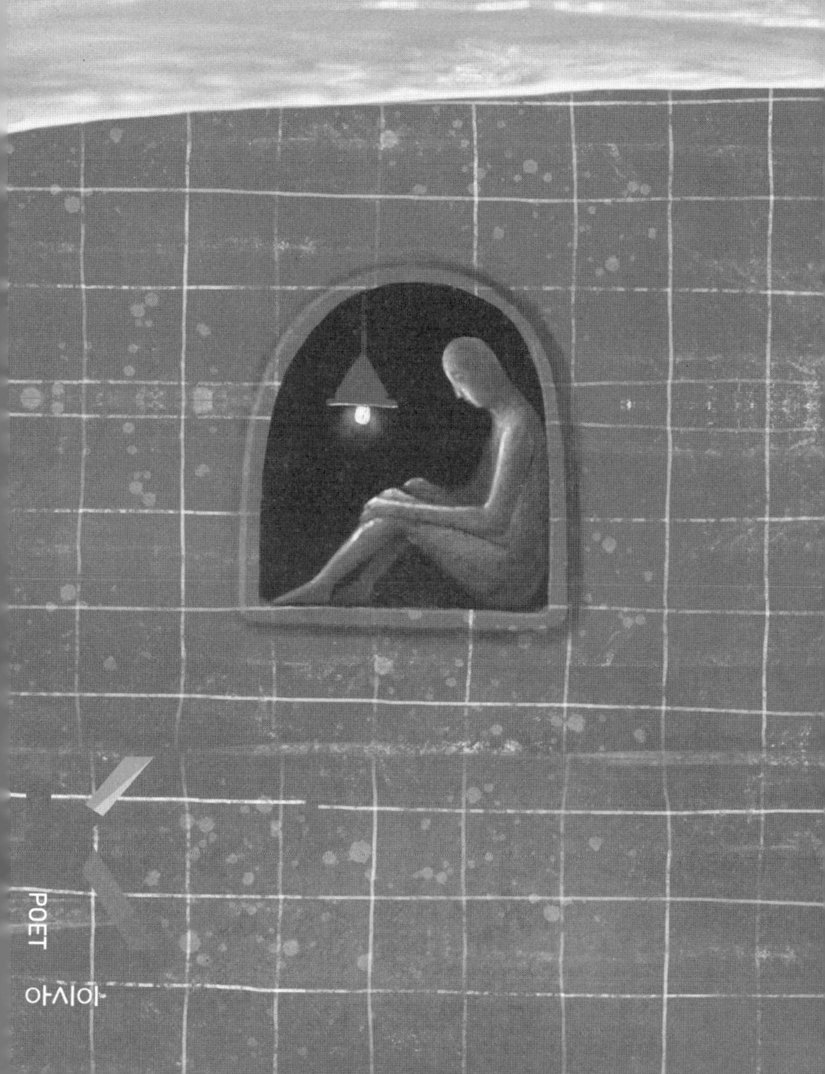

Contents

SUICIDE PARASITE

First Snow

On the day when first snow falls
you ask when is my birthday

I have had no birthday
since I left my mother
celebrating my birth
was poisoning my life

After leaving my home
any day with delightful snow on my body
is my birthday

Traditional Holiday

They put food on the low memorial table
along with a bowl of *tteokguk*[*]

when they kneel and bow will the dead
add years like the living?[**]

A young married couple kneels
before the photo on the table

The *tteokguk* is mushy but
their little child smiles

* Sliced rice cake soup

** Korean superstition says people add years by the number of bowls of *tteokguk* they eat on New Year's Day.

Time

They still put food on the low memorial table
along with a bowl of *tteokguk*

when they kneel and bow will the dead
add years like the living?

The elderly couple kneels
before the photo on the table

The *tteokguk* is mushy but
their little child always smiles

After Having My Molar Pulled

After the tooth is pulled my tongue probes the soft
gum I smell blood on the extracted gauze
Life and death are composed of such things
My flaccid flesh

As if petting a puppy my finger touches my gum
I've never known this sensation
Perhaps the reason to live is to experience new feelings
The generation who bites each day advises
to hide teeth well and bite fiercely when needed
The taste of blood is concealed
in soft words

They never lose what is theirs

I'm at the age where I neither want to live nor die
I go to the market to repurchase the lost tooth
but can't find the exact match
I think the phrase is "Clouds like bloody gauze"
A crying baby's face overlaps
the face of a nearly-dead elder pushing a stroller

I earn a living but wonder if I will eat food again
I must die in anxiety
The time for writing poetry has passed
and when night comes I shall honor all creatures
for I know the time is coming when they will beg

and wallow

in the dirt as they try to chew meat with their

gums

Suicide Parasite

There are flesh-eating insects Some people dote on these parasites while raising them They use various means to give them a high quality of flesh; they think when an owner dies, the bug kills itself in loyalty, so it is called the suicide parasite For the bugs, the owners drink, abuse women and scavenge for the best food; they listen to music and read books for snazzy pleasure; even poor people go crazy once they begin to raise the parasites Caring for the suicide parasite is more important than taking care of one's self Owners grow emaciated day by day but can't quit the only bug that loves and understands them The members of Suicide Parasite fan clubs celebrate their bugs to forget reality

Immediately before an owner dies, others swarm to lament or confirm their own health With the most pretending plaintive eyes they look upon the dying face It's not sure if they gaze at the owner or the parasite but they all burst into tears at the death Actually they clamor to occupy the bug When the soul loses all power the flesh grows tender and fatty It is the suicide parasite's favorite flesh to bore into At the moment of last eye contact with the owner, the parasite flees to another host and survives there Think about it People raise suicide bugs in order to drain the pleasure cup to the dregs The bugs grow fatter by gnawing on the owners No one tries to extract and squash them Why do people love these bugs to death? The parasites will carry on an immortal life with tenacious vitality much better than millions of sperm squirted into a uterus Suicide parasites miss their chance to commit suicide by constantly gnawing flesh They live endlessly cursing their owners for the gift of flesh

Love

Before cutting his birthday cake
he set on the table

he lights candles
and is surprised
by the sound
of his own clapping
laughing
the single man says
The hardest thing I should do
to love
myself:

extinguishing

by myself

the flame I ignited

Whenever I Want to Cry

"Well, we're good Don't worry"

"Is something going on?"

"Oh, you're busy I'll call later;

we're good"

Whenever she calls me

she seems to have something more to say

I lie down and close my eyes and think

Why did she call

her aging son?

"I'm ok as long as you are healthy."

When she closes her eyes, maybe she can't breathe

well like me;

is that why she called me?

Owl

An owl smashed the window and fell into the living room
with a head injury
bleeding on the floor and ruffling feathers
A rabbit bangs on the screen of its hutch
Exhausted, hungry and afraid
the owl glances from me to the rabbit

Clutching the owl's legs and folding its wings I get it into a cage
At night I can't sleep and speak to the owl
Where are you from? Do you feel death approaching?
You came here so your soul could rest?

I chop up a chicken from the fridge and toss pieces in the cage
Judging me with yellow eyes
it goes three days without touching the food

While I'm away the owl rends the flesh
it begins to gain weight and sleep well
The rabbit eats all day but grows emaciated
Upon hearing a bird call from the TV, the owl frees itself
scratches my arm, shakes the hutch in its talons
When I pry it away, the rabbit has pissed itself and died

You are not dead yet   From that day I watch the owl

Suffering from insomnia, I pull my hair out

Hey owl, insomnia makes me want to chew my own flesh

I can't sleep   I can't …

I open the window wide

put a chicken on the floor and go in my room

The owl's talons snatch the meat and it flies away

I run with arms outstretched and hurl myself into the window

large shards of glass shatter on the ground

When the free owl returns to its nest

to share meat with its own kind, it carries the smell of human

and the owl cries out as its fellows begin to tear it apart

I just want to live   why won't you recognize me?

I Cry in the Embrace of Snakes

I left the door ajar while I was gone
a swarm of snakes slid in and are now tangled
in my crumpled blanket
after rubbing their stomachs on my journal
the paper cold and white as snake eggs
they hide deep within the chest

No one catches snakes that lurk in the city
I sleep fearfully in the living room with the bedroom door closed
in my dreams swarms of snakes cross the threshold
sleek bodies crawl over manuscript pages
As if having a wet dream, I cry out

pull the blanket over my head and hear the hissing of my name

I wake up in tears but don't know whose tears they are

Tired, I find a damp shaded hole

and peek at the guests who plan to spend the winter here

But I will write a manuscript no one will read

I cannot help writing manuscripts no one can read

despite fatigue I must end this cohabitation

In my mirror a haggard wretch with sunken eyes

hammers umbrella handles upon snake bodies
that are dying with no chance to escape
I remember the thrill of watching snakes following
the smell of gunpowder at the military firing range
I've been starving for those elapsed seasons
as if hate and abandonment withers limbs and brews poison

Patterns appear on my prickling skin
and my hairs stand on end
shivering all over I pound the snakes to tatters
How could so many snakes live in the depths of

the city?

Like an old man who can only gum cooked rice
they and I accidentally hibernated in the same lair
and have no other place to go
unless we die
the pure and simple escape

I write and watch the white cold soul of sleet falling in the night
anger and abandonment led the snakes and me into another country
As if feeling the extreme emotion of embrace in Hell's arms
I smell bloody water resting in the space they had

occupied

Closing my eyes, sleek skins like naked women

dig into my flesh

I cry into my palms

shed clothes, shed limbs and slither

A hissing is heard as snakes cross the threshold

Flower's Sleep

A mother cow is licking
her just born baby

in deep sleep
lying
in dust-scattered
sunlight
in the flower bed
the calf
being licked
without getting up
lying
as the wind
gambols in the yard

under the clouds;

until a red flower blooms

on the tongue

of the calf

the mother cow

is licking

her dead baby

Dad, I Have No Money

I haven't eaten all day On the bus to Gwanghwamun I felt dizzy I was in a rush and broke out in a cold sweat as I walked I was starving The rain stopped and the fierce blue face of the sky made buildings gasp in a cold sweat I am dizzy I am so dizzy It's hard to write words I must do something to live There is no other motivation Life sings in gasps Dad, I, I feel hungry when I smell burning rubber You may say life is about stifling the nausea Some people cry standing others sleep standing others die standing Trees weep like people dying as they stand I don't want to live without a mouth Everyone lives only to survive All else is a lie Please, stop I look back I look back I don't try, try again I wanted to abandon people Then I became afraid they would judge me so I abandoned love instead Like a suspected criminal I live anxiously Anxiety turns me into food I haven't been caught yet, I couldn't be caught yet; that causes my tears, that rouses my fears Cool liquor remains in my hands Fire is in them I came back home with nausea The slums ignore my condition and illuminate my face I live here Home sweet home has no escape I should smile in appreciation as if treating an old friend I'm in a cold sweat I can't remember what I wrote maybe because of the medicine I could survive because I had no food today I always thank you Dad and again I don't blame you I made this

Faces

It rains heavily A swarm of people gather at the subway gate like refugees of the Great Depression Closing umbrellas they run downstairs to the platform In the subway a mugger takes a purse from a pregnant woman I should ignore this He looks people in their eyes People turn away I turn away too I get off the subway I should ignore this With a knife wound in her ribs the pregnant woman collapses behind the closing doors I should ignore this Some people walk to other cars

During morning rush hour frowns are walking I hurry through the underground corridors Thugs are stomping a guy at the transfer station Blood flows from the back of his trampled hand I should ignore this Blood follows my feet and seeps through a chink in the doors and stains my newspaper and splatters the lenses of my glasses

Disturbed, I throw the paper on the floor and trample it underfoot I should ignore this I should ignore this *Survive, whatever it takes* Whose voice is this? It comes from the air I cover my ears Whose voice was this? I get out at my station and walk protected by my umbrella Prostitutes loiter on the street

Princesses are drying their rain-soaked garments

Our glass house was destroyed It's easy to destroy a palace Soldiers hold hands with princesses and walk past ruined buildings with the uneasy eyes of birds Soldiers can't guard the palace They can only fire their guns when ordered Prostitutes clutch young soldiers to their chests as pigeons protect their eggs Police rush in to arrest the princesses and shove them into the patrol car Soldiers and police are brothers Young soldiers walk around searching for more princesses Bloody water follows the wheels of the patrol car

Broken windows, pink neon lights, city raining blood, forgotten princesses, floods of the Great

Depression, destroyed kingdom, prince who avoids rain but cries, heaven and hell for infidels, stabbed pregnant woman *You must survive*, man with blood-splattered glasses, *Everyone has the right to survive*, thugs stomping a guy, *I do this to survive, you son of a bitch*, blood-soaked newspaper, *must survive*, prostitutes who lost a palace. *You make us like this, asshole, just give me my money*, soldiers with no homes, *We can't go home if we don't survive*, voices filling the subways, voices pouring down like heavy rain

Nonchalant people look around They glance into faces washed by the rain

Heart

It had been a house of revolutionaries After a tip was received, several were hauled off in handcuffs When it happened, the house shrunk and stretched in fright It screamed Every day prostitutes went in and out of the glowing red house Drunken laughter was endless Coquettish voices never stopped It was a house of children born of loud trash revolutionaries and coquettish prostitutes; a paradise for ignoble beings It was a warehouse for bureaucrats Every day it would swell as if bursting after being filled with idle talk Shocked bureaucrats abandoned it and ran away so it became a house of gamblers, peasants, feminists and angels As it was caving in numerous people swarmed around   At first he was reticent   Then he declared we should keep running until right before it bursts

Crane

A crane lies on the gravel
with spread wings

My palms support its neck
but it doesn't raise its head

A fragment of fishing line hangs from the bill
dew dampens the wings
it couldn't fly away
or saw no use in fleeing

Holding water in cupped hands
I pour it through the bill onto the tongue

The lake's eyes sparkle
If one swallow means guilty
then atonement means death ···

Famished clouds close in
darkness spreads its wings
and blankets the unblinking crane

The Journal of a Fugitive

Years have passed since I fled the world
now no one recognizes me

Fugitives don't need tomorrows
if only today exists

drinking booze as if drinking water
drinking water as if drinking booze

If you don't love yourself
leave this place

I don't care about tomorrow
I don't care about the day after that

too much of anything is poison
I write about myself with that poison

but am deeply addicted to poison
so end up abandoning the self

Tonight seeing my face is shocking
the time has come to leave the me and turn myself in

Black Snake Swallowing White Snake

1

Professor, I caught a white snake Will you allow me to keep it?

2

I don't think it's a good idea to keep a venomous animal in the lab Professor, it is transforming It's shedding its skin The color will change An extraordinary research paper will come out of this Whenever I opened the glass cage the snake's color was darker The professor sometimes stroked the snake and gave food to it I hope it will eat less when it gets old After having shed its skin the snake didn't move for a few days Professor, it has been staring at me for the last few days Son, we can't pay your tuition Each time I had the phone call from home I cut off a finger and threw it to the snake Professor, I bought some meat for the snake from the market

When calendar pages fell like shed scales and the snake didn't darken any longer I sighed in the lab from which my desk had been removed, with the huge snake wrapped around my neck We can't fund your research any more; you eat too much I went back to my hometown, where elderly people were taking sunshine and squirming on the street, and in the middle of night I sneaked into my parents' house Don't cry, my son, you haven't changed a bit My mother crawled out from under the blanket and boiled water in the pot Air bubbles like eyes burst on the surface of water Mom, when I die I will vomit you from my entire body That's okay, son, eat ramen, you have to eat something, and all are dying, eating their own shed skin Laying her stomach on the floor she crawled back under the blanket

3

The snake carried on my back opens its eyes at the smell of ramen

sheds its skin

flicks its tongue toward my decrepit old mother

Son, eat ramen, you have to eat ⋯

Woman in a *Jokbal*[*] Restaurant

The woman scores chunks of raw *jokbal* from a plastic bucket
Feet fat as a pig's, she squats on her hams
and rinses blood from the knife with tap water
I start day-drinking, listening to the blood and water draining

Drinking *soju*[**] mixed with sunshine my body feels bright
Old veins washed in sunlight grow warm
She is focused on slicing as if carving her own slippered feet

* Steamed lower legs of pigs

** The most popular Korean liquor

and her knife knows no lethargy
because hunger frantically licks her flesh and bones
and the devil sucks her breast until it sags
I drink *soju* as if getting an injection of happiness
the sound of it filling my shot glass is soft
Ten dollars' worth of happiness   When she brings *anju*[*]
her pig feet-sized breasts are partly revealed by her sleeveless shirt
She grins   I smile and follow her
A lunatic, idiotic but talented
observes only one thing

* Food meant to be consumed while drinking alcohol

and with that thing, forgets all worldly reason

to stand fearlessly and daringly on the edge of a cliff

Whatever dreams she had had in her youth, failure and

abandonment accompanied her along her confident path

My breasts are still firm   Would you like to see?

Drunkenly she serves sliced meat and gives her breasts as well

In my eyes, the widow is a saint

How pathetic is a young fellow drunk in broad daylight!

Staggering, I think I hear someone scolding me

After mad drinking

I walk to my dark underground cave-like house and lie down

She's a failure but feels no fear of the world

She's fearless but wants direction and grabs the moment

Thousands of glaring stars with eyes rolling dizzily fall to the floor

Everyone Has Only Two Choices

I had no special talent and was raised by poor parents
People advised me to find a way to survive alone But
I didn't catch winter birds for food

I was a mediocre student but kept graduating
had a boring life knowing only workplace and home
Colleagues advised me to save relentlessly but sometimes
I loaned money while drinking with my hometown deadbeat friend

My time flowed toward unsettled people
I lost my job and avoided meeting anyone
But when I had the chance to drink
I didn't want to beg so I tried to pay the tab
with a frail voice and
lowered eyes retracing my footsteps

Confining myself, growing tired of people
I smiled despite my fear of myself
wanted to be confident but feared myself seeing me
wanting more and more intensely to steal bread
I didn't catch starving birds, didn't rat on colleagues

didn't trample others; I started to mumble and
realized I was neither vicious nor strong, just weak

I walked down night streets glancing around like a nervous bird
blaming myself for no talent
leaning toward fear
Birds sang for me as I shivered in the cold, friends advised me
and my family waited for a son who could not return home

Taking Vitality Potions My Father Left

My father is being treated for liver cancer
At morning and night he drinks a vitality potion
The packets he doesn't finish are piled
one by one in a bag
for me

After returning to Seoul I instantly sleep
The next morning I call around
to apologize for deadlines I've missed
After going home I notice the drink packets

I heard Dad often forgets to take them
and falls asleep
He gave them to me

saying they're good for my health

and they also cure hangovers

Gradually I hear

wind flowing in the air

leaves descending

sounds that weren't heard during childhood

A Day Before

Behind his back a dead man was
standing and watching him carry packages

When he was terribly fatigued and collapsed
did he feel sad?
Before sleeping I write down
what I wanted

At night with no time to feel sad I sleep deeply
A dead man is standing, watching me
even during sleep
I can feel it

The next day, or the day after that

I know I should stop but

when I wake up

I write a line, thinking this is the last one

No matter how much I suffer

my mind is never being trained

The dead man wipes my forehead

POET'S NOTE

Boat of Ice

In my childhood, I have experienced chopping river ice into a big square with an ax and a rock. I stood on the big ice cube and poled it across the frozen river. At the edge of the opposite riverbank, cold and clear water was flowing under the thinly frozen ice, and bivalves with shells closed tight were in the freshwater. Afraid of melting ice, I rushed to push my floe with the pole, and the action accelerated the melting. When the ice cracked, I fell into the water. I was afraid of my mother scolding me, so I made a fire at the riverside and dried my wet clothes. Doing it, I singed my clothes and my eyebrows.

Sometimes I loaded the ice-built boat with firewood. People don't believe my story because I am too young to be of that generation, but my home was in the secluded countryside and my family was poor. We had no reason to spend money for charcoal since we lived by a mountain full of firewood. Drunken men of the village staggered on the snow-piled path in the middle of the day. On traditional market days, they had a second round of drinking in the market and walked into the deep valley. They would sleep in the levees of rice paddies. In the next morning, some lucky ones were found alive, and others were dead in fluttering beautiful snowflakes.

There were people who died from heatstroke, and others drowned in floods. There was a woman who was swept away by her tragic life. Her alcoholic husband had abused her, and one day, she was so angry with him, she drank a lot, and killed herself by taking bottled pesticide. The woman, who tried to put up stiff resistance and restore her right to live as a human, not just as a woman, looked beautiful to my eyes. In the face of death, there is no right and wrong, or ethics, or moral compass. Those people's days were full of fierce battles creating wild waves. They were swept away by the waves, driven to the edges of rivers, and plunged over the waterfalls, being pushed by their extreme angst.

I grew up and cut my eyeteeth in that village. Now, however, the blade of my life is dull with the dirt on it and more and more I feel empty.

Without knowing when the ice-built boat will melt, I pole over the ice, feeling insecure. Even if it is a game at the risk of my life, the thrill makes me stay on the boat and I don't know when I will stop this journey.

My grandmother died in the angry waves of the river of life, my father was drifted over the edge of the river, my siblings watched the flood innocently, and my mother crawled over the edge of the river after struggling in the waves and took care of her family. There was a person who hesitated as he witnessed all of those occurrences. Now, he murmurs regretting his hesitation at that time. Murmuring makes him feel guilty, so he cries.

The crying person simply lives a materialistic life without blaming anyone except himself. He fails to wash away the sins of his past hesitation and his present murmurs and lives crying for mercy. Why did he hesitate at that time? Why does he murmur as he summons the past? Why does he write down the memory of hesitation as he murmurs and begs for mercy? He thinks of the drunken village guys staggering while being scolded. He thinks of a man who walked into a blizzard and fell asleep with his peaceful face in the embrace of the snowstorm.

THE POET'S ESSAY

A Person Crossed the River and Left His Family Behind

I was born in a remote village in North Chungcheong Province. The Geum River flows through my hometown. In summer, I used to swim all day long in the river or catch fish and sometimes tadpoles until dinnertime. The sky glowed in the setting sun above the river and I sometimes caught fish till late at night.

Unlike my generation, I had five siblings and my family lived with my paternal grandmother. My mother got a job working for a rest stop food court before I entered elementary school, and I used to walk there to meet my mother in the evening. Sometimes I went there with my younger brother and sometimes with my older sister. While I walked on the path, impatient to see her, I was fearful of something popping out of the darkness.

When I was playing with kids by the river till late, my mother stood at the entrance of the village and yelled my name, informing me dinner was ready. Then, I yelled back loudly, saying I was going home right away.

My mother was the main breadwinner in my poor family. My father's farming was only a means of self-sufficiency.

This autobiographical poetry book honestly shows about my life. My mother crossed the bridge to go to work and the river flowing under the bridge separated me from my mother. Perhaps, the feeling of my desolation started to grow at that time.

When I entered middle school, every morning I walked to the bus stop to go to school by crossing the bridge my mother used. There were only twenty students in my elementary grade. Going to a big middle school in town was the first city-type experience to me, and it was scary to a countryside boy like me.

My mother was strong with the ability to earn a living, while my father was a tender-minded person. He only graduated elementary school but liked to study and such manual labor of farming in hills and fields was too hard for him. He was often drunk and had a pessimistic approach to his life.

In my adolescence, I found out a sad story about my family.

My paternal grandfather was also a poor farmer but was very gentle and worked endlessly all his life. However, he had a second wife, who lived nearby. My grandmother hated him, and my father had a lot of stress because he had to encounter his half-sisters and brothers in the same village as he took care of his mother.

Grandmother died in the middle of summer the

year I entered elementary school. She was over eighty when she died. She had worked hard for life without having days off and a decent meal. She often said she would like to die and finally ended her life by drinking bottled pesticide. What I had worried about really happened.

My family couldn't afford rice, so we ate boiled barley. In winter, we built a simple container to keep sweet potatoes in our bedroom. Baked or boiled sweet potatoes substituted for one meal everyday and the container became light as days passed. The container was empty when spring sunshine grew warm.

In the hunger and the countryside life, quite different from the life of my generation, my poetic seeds were slowly growing.

Sometimes my maternal grandmother came from far away to see my mother, her only daughter, by taking a train and walking a long way. She sometimes told me, "It would have been good if your older brother hadn't died." If she hadn't said that, I wouldn't have known I had another brother.

When I was a high school student, one day I heard my parents having a big argument because my mother found a childhood photo of my dead brother in my father's wallet. Crying, she tore the photo into pieces and threw them in the trash. He just watched without saying anything.

When the brother was in elementary school, he drowned in the river while playing with friends. I don't remember who told the story, but I think that incident was the biggest cause that gave my family a hard time. Since then, my father drank every day and he lived for a few years out of his mind. When he drank too much, sometimes he completely lost his memory. My mother looked after him by taking him to different hospitals, including acupuncture clinics. At last he could live a normal life, but his life was always clouded with gloom.

Time passed and my parents had more children. To go to the field for working, they had to pass the road in front of the elementary school my brother had attended. The school bell sound was heard in the field. There wasn't a single day when they didn't think about their dead son, and if they tried to forget, the scenery and the bell summoned memories of their son. Who could imagine the pain they felt every day seeing the school? When I was a child, I didn't know how much they suffered from the great pain of loss, but now I can kind of understand it.

Around when I graduated from elementary school, my older sisters took factory jobs in Busan. One of them left on a shuttle bus for a shoe factory with some classmates on the day of middle school graduation. When I was older, I could learn through records like movies how much they were abused in factories.

I am the fifth among six siblings with a younger brother. When I was growing up, naturally I received much attention from my family. I felt responsible for my family and at the same time had the desire to write poems. But I knew early that writing poems was exactly the opposite of what they expected from me.

In high school, I fell in love with literature and began to write poems. In my poems, I expressed my dissatisfaction with the situation of my family, resentment toward the world, and the feeling of powerlessness. Thinking about my family who placed their hopes on me, I felt guilty, but I couldn't help writing poems. If I hadn't written poems, I couldn't have had a normal life, blaming some unknown existence.

What does writing poems mean? Is it important to become a renowned poet? It is natural that artists from any fields want to create great art. When they fail to make excellent works, they will feel so frustrated.

But now, I think the action of writing itself is important, although I can't get any riches and honor. Painting pictures on paper by melting my agony, whether to blame myself, or to love and understand myself, is the base of poetry and inside the base, the seed of poetry will start to grow.

COMMENTARY

K

POET

Attitude of Living in a Semi-Basement Apartment

Park Dong-eok(Critic)

What is the origin of Kim Seong-gyu's stories? This is a query about the root of his agony that his poems convey, and in fact an inquiry about observing his agony from a distance. In many stories, life is commonly portrayed as an adventure with a string of choices as it advances toward the future. However, we are living in an age where life at work and home has become a substitution for adventure. Mass media has set up the clichéd storyline of people suffering from adventurous hardships of decision-making at workplaces until they return home, and the story ends smoothly with the scene of family members giving a warm welcome to the hard worker.

There are lives that don't have many choices from the beginning. To these people, going back home means failure. Their life is all about relentless escape, like a family living in a poor semi-basement apartment, or slaughtered pigs to be buried after contracting a contagious disease. Leaving their home is the only means for them to survive. In his poetry book *When Will Heaven Collect Broken Men?* (Changbi Publishers, 2013), Kim depicts characters that have only two choices: moving forward or falling. When they are desperate with no place to rely on, they must hang on the cliff or be buried after falling. They live in "one room dug underground" that is termed "the kingdom of pains" in the poem given the same title as the book.

Kim seems to enlighten us about people who can upgrade their life only to the height of their own graves. This is reminiscent of the movie *Parasite* directed by Bong Joon-ho. In the movie, a semi-basement apartment is contrasted with a luxurious mansion with a garden, being operated as allegories of the gap between the rich and poor. The family from the semi-basement apartment could belong to the rich family living in the mansion by completely concealing their identities and disguising themselves as different people — by leaving themselves. The reason the film could gain huge popularity around the world was perhaps because it succeeded in sarcastically and humorously describing the self-abandonment.

Meanwhile, Kim testifies to reality with his secret voice. To get sunshine, a man in the semi-basement room must escape from there by painfully abandoning himself, while people living above the ground can naturally earn sunlight. The escaped person narrates, "I sold my heart dirt-cheap / Sitting in a seat at the corner of a bar, I think of the singing heart" (from "Crying Heart"). An extremely poor person sells the self at a low price to become an ordinary person. Singing only means a nostalgic action toward the lost self. The person's existential angst comes from self-abandonment more than from poverty. The person lives a sorrowful life, pretending to be calm and ignoring his poor family and the self. The record about the person's life is close to a testimony of silence.

In this new collection of 20 poems, we should focus on the weight of silence hidden beyond words. In the poem "First Snow," Kim says, "I have had no birthday / since I left my mother / celebrating my birth / was poisoning my life."

If we translate these lines literally, Kim seems to express a deep attachment to his mother, and any delights he feels without his mother are meaningless. But it is naïve to say he only longs for home where his mother lives, because his despair arising from a miserably poor life is rooted in the home where poverty awaits, although he has much affection for his mother. When we draw such despair from beyond the context, we can realize the true weight of the line, "and my family waited for a son who could not return home" ("Everyone Has Only Two Choices"). What did he leave behind in order to escape from hunger? How does his family feel, waiting for the son who won't return?

A desperately poor person sells the self cheaply in order to survive, selling his blood or prostituting his pen. Because he cannot afford to love himself, he prefers "extinguishing / by myself / the flame I ignited" ("Love") to falling in love with someone else. In that sense, it is not surprising that Kim Seong-gyu contemplates death, the exit of life.

Here, death should be interpreted with the concept of transcendentalism. As seen from the lines "for I know the time is coming when they will beg and wallow / in the dirt as they try to chew meat with their gums" ("After Having My Molar Pulled"), to the person who has no other choice, death is imagining a negative theology that creates new choices by attempting to discover what cannot be said.

Compared to his earlier books that concentrate on the pursuit of death by the poet himself, in this book, contemplation of death and the pursuit of death belong to others. In "Traditional Holiday" and "Time," the married couple meditates on death before the memorial table. The pursuit of death in "Suicide Parasite" is replaced with an insect surviving inside a person's body. This implies that Kim is turning his eyes from his own despair to that of others; that is to say, he is shifting the gravitational center of lamentation from himself to others. Such a decision is rooted in his mother. When we read the lines "When she closes her eyes, maybe she can't breathe well like me; / is that why she called me?" ("Whenever I Want to Cry"), we notice that his mother saves her words so as not to burden her son with her pains, and the son has already comprehended his mother's unsaid words. Suppressing groans, they simply ask after each other, hang on the warmth of their voices, and give hugs from a distance.

In the poem "Owl," the question from the line "I just want to live   why won't you recognize me?" seems like the source of his loss that drives the poet into writing poetry. We can understand this question by thinking about the paradox that some people can survive only by giving themselves away. Sometimes we do what we really don't want to do. If this happens once in a while, we can dismiss it as the accumulation of experiences. However, if it happens all the time and we should keep living a pretentious life, our life will be full of distress. Writing poetry comforts a betrayed life as described in lines "sleek bodies crawl over manuscript pages / As if having a wet dream, I cry out" ("I Cry in the Embrace of Snakes") where snakes record the poet's existence and "I" am the shed skin that remains.

Because of the discrepancy between the true self and the ego, the ego needs a symbol in order to be revealed. In the poem "Suicide Parasite," why does Kim use a metaphor of a bug for the death wish? At first glance, the suicide parasite sounds like suicidal impulses that torment humans. But this is not all. In the poem "I cry in the Embrace of Snakes," the speaker is "in the embrace" of snakes because he can't deal with his loneliness alone. Likewise, the speaker in "Suicide Parasite" imagines the cohabitation with the bug as he imagines the parasite that bores into his flesh.

The "I" is too wide to manage, so it desires the insect to live inside its existence, the "me" full of desolation and silence. In this imagination, solitude is interpreted as agony that bores into the flesh. In fact, Kim Seong-gyu says all people live by enduring solitude and this idea appears in the line "Nonchalant people look around They glance into faces washed by the rain" ("Faces"). My solitude and yours are not the same as individuals who have their own wet faces. Thinking in that way, we can say the line "Gradually I hear" ("Taking Vitality Potions My Father Left") and your tormenting silence is felt. We also can say that we will endure as much as you endure and that now "The dead man wipes my forehead" ("A Day Before").

Solitude, screams and groans seep into the silence of empty packets of vitality potions or unreachable beckoning of the dead. The "faces washed by the rain" are silent and individual. In the silence, the poet strains his ears to hear what can't be heard, so he resembles "A lunatic, idiotic but talented / observes only one thing / and with that thing, forgets all worldly reason / to stand fearlessly and daringly on the edge of a cliff" ("Woman in a *Jokbal* Restaurant"). The poet is a person who "realized I was neither vicious nor strong, just weak" ("Everyone Has Only Two Choices") and survives through self-deception. However, he doesn't ignore failures, because he knows what a miserable life feels like. In the shadow of his semi-basement room, he looks up at things that are collapsing as he reflects deeply on them and daringly stands up under the low ceiling.

WHAT THEY SAY ABOUT KIM SEONG-GYU

K

POET

Kim Seong-gyu's poems reveal the scars of people living in the brutal and fierce world. They are sad portrayals of shocking and bizarre lives surviving in the nauseating world, of you and me walking through a minefield, or of a woman in sudden labor who drops a watermelon while treading heavily uphill to her home.

Kang Woo-seok (Poet)

The unconvincing mechanisms and uncharted territories Kim Seong-gyu goes through appear in his poems allegorically. Although his allegorical concept doesn't always work successfully, it performs a significant role to view the other side of the world of lyrical verse he pursues, of his hardships and the affection he has toward his family and hometown.

Han Gi-wook (Critic)

K-POET
Suicide Parasite

Written by Kim Seong-gyu
Translated by YoungShil Ji and Daniel Todd Parker
Published by ASIA Publishers
Address 445, Hoedong-gil, Paju-si, Gyeonggi-do, Korea
Tel (8231).955.7958
Fax (8231).955.7956
Email bookasia@hanmail.net
Homepage Address www.bookasia.org

ISBN 979-11-5662-317-5 (set) | 979-11-5662-544-5 (04810)

First published in Korea by ASIA Publishers 2021

This book is published with the support of the Literature Translation Institute of Korea (LTI Korea).

바이링궐 에디션 한국 대표 소설

한국문학의 가장 중요하고 첨예한 문제의식을 가진 작가들의 대표작을 주제별로 선정!
하버드 한국학 연구원 및 세계 각국의 한국문학 전문 번역진이 참여한 번역 시리즈!
미국 하버드대학교와 컬럼비아대학교 동아시아학과, 캐나다 브리티시컬럼비아대학교 아시아학과 등 해외 대학에서 교재로 채택!

바이링궐 에디션 한국 대표 소설 set 1

분단 Division

01 병신과 머저리-**이청준** The Wounded-**Yi Cheong-jun**
02 어둠의 혼-**김원일** Soul of Darkness-**Kim Won-il**
03 순이삼촌-**현기영** Sun-i Samch'on-**Hyun Ki-young**
04 엄마의 말뚝 1-**박완서** Mother's Stake I-**Park Wan-suh**
05 유형의 땅-**조정래** The Land of the Banished-**Jo Jung-rae**

산업화 Industrialization

06 무진기행-**김승옥** Record of a Journey to Mujin-**Kim Seung-ok**
07 삼포 가는 길-**황석영** The Road to Sampo-**Hwang Sok-yong**
08 아홉 켤레의 구두로 남은 사내-**윤흥길** The Man Who Was Left as Nine Pairs of Shoes-**Yun Heung-gil**
09 돌아온 우리의 친구-**신상웅** Our Friend's Homecoming-**Shin Sang-ung**
10 원미동 시인-**양귀자** The Poet of Wŏnmi-dong-**Yang Kwi-ja**

여성 Women

11 중국인 거리-**오정희** Chinatown-**Oh Jung-hee**
12 풍금이 있던 자리-**신경숙** The Place Where the Harmonium Was-**Shin Kyung-sook**
13 하나코는 없다-**최윤** The Last of Hanak'o-**Ch'oe Yun**
14 인간에 대한 예의-**공지영** Human Decency-**Gong Ji-young**
15 빈처-**은희경** Poor Man's Wife-**Eun Hee-kyung**

바이링궐 에디션 한국 대표 소설 set 2

자유 Liberty

16 필론의 돼지-**이문열** Pilon's Pig-**Yi Mun-yol**
17 슬로우 불릿-**이대환** Slow Bullet-**Lee Dae-hwan**
18 직선과 독가스-**임철우** Straight Lines and Poison Gas-**Lim Chul-woo**
19 깃발-**홍희담** The Flag-**Hong Hee-dam**
20 새벽 출정-**방현석** Off to Battle at Dawn-**Bang Hyeon-seok**

사랑과 연애 Love and Love Affairs

21 별을 사랑하는 마음으로-**윤후명** With the Love for the Stars-**Yun Hu-myong**
22 목련공원-**이승우** Magnolia Park-**Lee Seung-u**
23 칼에 찔린 자국-**김인숙** Stab-**Kim In-suk**
24 회복하는 인간-**한강** Convalescence-**Han Kang**
25 트렁크-**정이현** In the Trunk-**Jeong Yi-hyun**

남과 북 South and North

26 판문점-**이호철** Panmunjom-**Yi Ho-chol**
27 수난 이대-**하근찬** The Suffering of Two Generations-**Ha Geun-chan**
28 분지-**남정현** Land of Excrement-**Nam Jung-hyun**
29 봄 실상사-**정도상** Spring at Silsangsa Temple-**Jeong Do-sang**
30 은행나무 사랑-**김하기** Gingko Love-**Kim Ha-kee**

바이링궐 에디션 한국 대표 소설 set 3

서울 Seoul

31 눈사람 속의 검은 항아리-**김소진** The Dark Jar within the Snowman-**Kim So-jin**
32 오후, 가로지르다-**하성란** Traversing Afternoon-**Ha Seong-nan**
33 나는 봉천동에 산다-**조경란** I Live in Bongcheon-dong-**Jo Kyung-ran**
34 그렇습니까? 기린입니다-**박민규** Is That So? I'm A Giraffe-**Park Min-gyu**
35 성탄특선-**김애란** Christmas Specials-**Kim Ae-ran**

전통 Tradition

36 무자년의 가을 사흘-**서정인** Three Days of Autumn, 1948-**Su Jung-in**
37 유자소전-**이문구** A Brief Biography of Yuja-**Yi Mun-gu**
38 향기로운 우물 이야기-**박범신** The Fragrant Well-**Park Bum-shin**
39 월행-**송기원** A Journey under the Moonlight-**Song Ki-won**
40 협죽도 그늘 아래-**성석제** In the Shade of the Oleander-**Song Sok-ze**

아방가르드 Avant-garde

41 아겔다마-**박상륭** Akeldama-**Park Sang-ryoong**
42 내 영혼의 우물-**최인석** A Well in My Soul-**Choi In-seok**
43 당신에 대해서-**이인성** On You-**Yi In-seong**
44 회색 時-**배수아** Time In Gray-**Bae Su-ah**
45 브라운 부인-**정영문** Mrs. Brown-**Jung Young-moon**

바이링궐 에디션 한국 대표 소설 set 4

디아스포라 Diaspora

46 속옷-**김남일** Underwear-**Kim Nam-il**
47 상하이에 두고 온 사람들-**공선옥** People I Left in Shanghai-**Gong Sun-ok**
48 모두에게 복된 새해-**김연수** Happy New Year to Everyone-**Kim Yeon-su**
49 코끼리-**김재영** The Elephant-**Kim Jae-young**
50 먼지별-**이경** Dust Star-**Lee Kyung**

가족 Family

51 혜자의 눈꽃-**천승세** Hye-ja's Snow-Flowers-**Chun Seung-sei**
52 아베의 가족-**전상국** Ahbe's Family-**Jeon Sang-guk**
53 문 앞에서-**이동하** Outside the Door-**Lee Dong-ha**
54 그리고, 축제-**이혜경** And Then the Festival-**Lee Hye-kyung**
55 봄밤-**권여선** Spring Night-**Kwon Yeo-sun**

유머 Humor

56 오늘의 운세-**한창훈** Today's Fortune-**Han Chang-hoon**
57 새-**전성태** Bird-**Jeon Sung-tae**
58 밀수록 다시 가까워지는-**이기호** So Far, and Yet So Near-**Lee Ki-ho**
59 유리방패-**김중혁** The Glass Shield-**Kim Jung-hyuk**
60 전당포를 찾아서-**김종광** The Pawnshop Chase-**Kim Chong-kwang**

바이링궐 에디션 한국 대표 소설 set 5

관계 Relationship

61 도둑견습 - **김주영** Robbery Training-**Kim Joo-young**
62 사랑하라, 희망 없이 - **윤영수** Love, Hopelessly-**Yun Young-su**
63 봄날 오후, 과부 셋 - **정지아** Spring Afternoon, Three Widows-**Jeong Ji-a**
64 유턴 지점에 보물지도를 묻다 - **윤성희** Burying a Treasure Map at the U-turn-**Yoon Sung-hee**
65 쁘이거나 쯔이거나 - **백가흠** Puy, Thuy, Whatever-**Paik Ga-huim**

일상의 발견 Discovering Everyday Life

66 나는 음식이다 - **오수연** I Am Food-**Oh Soo-yeon**
67 트럭 - **강영숙** Truck-**Kang Young-sook**
68 통조림 공장 - **편혜영** The Canning Factory-**Pyun Hye-young**
69 꽃 - **부희령** Flowers-**Pu Hee-ryoung**
70 피의일요일 - **윤이형** BloodySunday-**Yun I-hyeong**

금기와 욕망 Taboo and Desire

71 북소리 - **송영** Drumbeat-**Song Yong**
72 발칸의 장미를 내게 주었네 - **정미경** He Gave Me Roses of the Balkans-**Jung Mi-kyung**
73 아무도 돌아오지 않는 밤 - **김숨** The Night Nobody Returns Home-**Kim Soom**
74 젓가락여자 - **천운영** Chopstick Woman-**Cheon Un-yeong**
75 아직 일어나지 않은 일 - **김미월** What Has Yet to Happen-**Kim Mi-wol**

바이링궐 에디션 한국 대표 소설 set 6

운명 Fate

76 언니를 놓치다 - **이경자** Losing a Sister-**Lee Kyung-ja**
77 아들 - **윤정모** Father and Son-**Yoon Jung-mo**
78 명두 - **구효서** Relics-**Ku Hyo-seo**
79 모독 - **조세희** Insult-**Cho Se-hui**
80 화요일의 강 - **손홍규** Tuesday River-**Son Hong-gyu**

미의 사제들 Aesthetic Priests

81 고수 - **이외수** Grand Master-**Lee Oisoo**
82 말을 찾아서 - **이순원** Looking for a Horse-**Lee Soon-won**
83 상춘곡 - **윤대녕** Song of Everlasting Spring-**Youn Dae-nyeong**
84 삭매와 자미 - **김별아** Sakmae and Jami-**Kim Byeol-ah**
85 저만치 혼자서 - **김훈** Alone Over There-**Kim Hoon**

식민지의 벌거벗은 자들 The Naked in the Colony

86 감자 - **김동인** Potatoes-**Kim Tong-in**
87 운수 좋은 날 - **현진건** A Lucky Day-**Hyŏn Chin'gŏn**
88 탈출기 - **최서해** Escape-**Ch'oe So-hae**
89 과도기 - **한설야** Transition-**Han Seol-ya**
90 지하촌 - **강경애** The Underground Village-**Kang Kyŏng-ae**

바이링궐 에디션 한국 대표 소설 set 7

백치가 된 식민지 지식인 Colonial Intellectuals Turned "Idiots"

91 날개 - **이상** Wings-**Yi Sang**
92 김 강사와 T 교수 - **유진오** Lecturer Kim and Professor T-**Chin-O Yu**
93 소설가 구보씨의 일일 - **박태원** A Day in the Life of Kubo the Novelist-**Pak Taewon**
94 비 오는 길 - **최명익** Walking in the Rain-**Ch'oe Myŏngik**
95 빛 속에 - **김사량** Into the Light-**Kim Sa-ryang**

한국의 잃어버린 얼굴 Traditional Korea's Lost Faces

96 봄·봄 – **김유정** Spring, Spring–**Kim Yu-jeong**
97 벙어리 삼룡이 – **나도향** Samnyong the Mute–**Na Tohyang**
98 달밤 – **이태준** An Idiot's Delight–**Yi T'ae-jun**
99 사랑손님과 어머니 – **주요섭** Mama and the Boarder–**Chu Yo-sup**
100 갯마을 – **오영수** Seaside Village–**Oh Yeongsu**

해방 전후(前後) Before and After Liberation

101 소망 – **채만식** Juvesenility–**Ch'ae Man-Sik**
102 두 파산 – **염상섭** Two Bankruptcies–**Yom Sang-Seop**
103 풀잎 – **이효석** Leaves of Grass–**Lee Hyo-seok**
104 맥 – **김남천** Barley–**Kim Namch'on**
105 꺼삐딴 리 – **전광용** Kapitan Ri–**Chŏn Kwangyong**

전후(戰後) Korea After the Korean War

106 소나기 – **황순원** The Cloudburst–**Hwang Sun-Won**
107 등신불 – **김동리** Tŭngsin-bul–**Kim Tong-ni**
108 요한 시집 – **장용학** The Poetry of John–**Chang Yong-hak**
109 비 오는 날 – **손창섭** Rainy Days–**Son Chang-sop**
110 오발탄 – **이범선** A Stray Bullet–**Lee Beomseon**

K-픽션 한국 젊은 소설

최근에 발표된 단편소설 중 가장 우수하고 흥미로운 작품을 엄선하여 출간하는 〈K-픽션〉은 한국문학의 생생한 현장을 국내외 독자들과 실시간으로 공유하고자 기획되었습니다. 원작의 재미와 품격을 최대한 살린 〈K-픽션〉 시리즈는 매 계절마다 새로운 작품을 선보입니다.

001 버핏과의 저녁 식사-**박민규** Dinner with Buffett-**Park Min-gyu**
002 아르판-**박형서** Arpan-**Park hyoung su**
003 애드벌룬-**손보미** Hot Air Balloon-**Son Bo-mi**
004 나의 클린트 이스트우드-**오한기** My Clint Eastwood-**Oh Han-ki**
005 이베리아의 전갈-**최민우** Dishonored-**Choi Min-woo**
006 양의 미래-**황정은** Kong's Garden-**Hwang Jung-eun**
007 대니-**윤이형** Danny-**Yun I-hyeong**
008 퇴근-**천명관** Homecoming-**Cheon Myeong-kwan**
009 옥화-**금희** Ok-hwa-**Geum Hee**
010 시차-**백수린** Time Difference-**Baik Sou linne**
011 올드 맨 리버-**이장욱** Old Man River-**Lee Jang-wook**
012 권순찬과 착한 사람들-**이기호** Kwon Sun-chan and Nice People-**Lee Ki-ho**
013 알바생 자르기-**장강명** Fired-**Chang Kangmyoung**
014 어디로 가고 싶으신가요-**김애란** Where Would You Like To Go?-**Kim Ae-ran**
015 세상에서 가장 비싼 소설-**김민정** The World's Most Expensive Novel-**Kim Min-jung**
016 체스의 모든 것-**김금희** Everything About Chess-**Kim Keum-hee**
017 할로윈-**정한아** Halloween-**Chung Han-ah**
018 그 여름-**최은영** The Summer-**Choi Eunyoung**
019 어느 피씨주의자의 종생기-**구병모** The Story of P.C.-**Gu Byeong-mo**
020 모르는 영역-**권여선** An Unknown Realm-**Kwon Yeo-sun**
021 4월의 눈-**손원평** April Snow-**Sohn Won-pyung**
022 서우-**강화길** Seo-u-**Kang Hwa-gil**
023 가출-**조남주** Run Away-**Cho Nam-joo**
024 연애의 감정학-**백영옥** How to Break Up Like a Winner-**Baek Young-ok**
025 창모-**우다영** Chang-mo-**Woo Da-young**
026 검은 방-**정지아** The Black Room-**Jeong Ji-a**
027 도쿄의 마야-**장류진** Maya in Tokyo-**Jang Ryu-jin**
028 홀리데이 홈-**편혜영** Holiday Home-**Pyun Hye-young**
029 해피 투게더-**서장원** Happy Together-**Seo Jang-won**